This book belongs to

_____

HELPING KIDS
LIVE GOD'S WAY

Right Choices

KENNETH N. TAYLOR

illustrated by
Kathryn
Shoemaker

TYNDALE
KIDS

Tyndale House Publishers, Inc.
Wheaton, Illinois

Visit Tyndale's exciting Web site at www.tyndale.com

Other children's books by Kenneth N. Taylor:

My First Bible in Pictures
My First Bible Words: A Kid's Devotional
Everything a Child Should Know about God
Stories about Jesus
Ken Taylor's Favorite Bible Stories
Big Thoughts for Little People
Giant Steps for Little People
Good News for Little People
Wise Words for Little People
The Bible in Pictures for Little Eyes (Moody Press)
Devotions for the Children's Hour (Moody Press)

Edited by Betty Free
Designed by Catherine Bergstrom

Scripture quotations on pages 8–44, 50, and 54 are based on *The Living Bible,* copyright © 1971. Used by permission of Tyndale House Publishers, Inc., Wheaton, Illinois 60189. All rights reserved.

Scripture quotations on pages 46–48, 52, and 56–58 are taken from the *Holy Bible,* New Living Translation, copyright © 1996. Used by permission of Tyndale House Publishers, Inc., Wheaton, Illinois 60189. All rights reserved.

Library of Congress Cataloging-in-Publication Data

Taylor, Kenneth Nathaniel.
   Right choices / Kenneth N. Taylor ; illustrations by Kathryn E. Shoemaker.
      p. cm.
   Summary: Twenty-six entries discuss wrong choices, such as lying, pride, and looking at "bad" television, and right choices, such as thankfulness, obedience, and talking often to God. Each entry includes questions, a little prayer, and a Bible verse to learn.
   ISBN 0-8423-5299-6 (alk. paper)
   1. Ethics—Juvenile literature.   2. Children—Conduct of life. [1. Prayer books and devotions.   2. Christian life.] I. Shoemaker, Kathryn E., ill.
II. Title.
BJ1631.T4   1998
241—dc21   98-15769

Printed in Mexico

05   04   03
7   6   5   4   3   2

A Word to Parents (and Grandparents)

Little eyes and ears are powerful. What they see and hear at an early age can deeply affect their entire life. "Give me a child until he is five years old," it has been said, "and I will have directed his life forever." How important it is, then, to fill little minds with life-changing thoughts.

The purpose of this book is to teach small children about Christian living—that is, how to be good! This is one of the great themes of the Bible, and it is very important for little children to be taught right from wrong (as well as simple courtesy and good manners).

A word about the wonderful artwork is in order. In addition to their teaching value, the pictures are filled with ladybug surprises. For instance, how many ladybugs can you and your child find on the cover? (I see one there!) Many ladybugs are hiding in the other illustrations throughout the book.

The questions are a very important part of each lesson also. Questions that are thought-provoking but not hard to answer have an important role in the learning process.

And please don't skip the Bible verses. Children will learn them easily and will keep them in their mind and heart for life. Picture books are soon outgrown, but Bible verses memorized in childhood last for a lifetime.

May God use this book to help your child, grandchild, or young friend grow in the grace of our Lord Jesus Christ.

Kenneth N. Taylor

Some things are RIGHT
And some are WRONG.
And none are in between.
So whether you
Guess right or wrong
Will very soon be seen!

Do you like guessing games? It is fun to guess, especially when you are right!

In this little book of yours, you can look at each picture and guess whether the children are doing what is right or what is wrong. Then you can think about things you do and whether it is good or not good to do those things.

God is glad when we are good. But he is unhappy with us when we are bad. So ask him to help you always do what is right and good. Then God will be glad, and other people will be glad, and you will be glad too.

A question to answer: In the picture, what book are the children reading? (I think it is this book of yours!)

Look: There are pictures of ladybugs on every page! See if you can find them!

It's time to be thankful!
Thank God for your lunch,
And thank him for dinner
And breakfast and brunch.

The children in the picture are thanking God for their food. Many children in the world don't have enough to eat. They are hungry all the time. But we have good breakfasts and lunches and suppers, and sometimes even snacks in between. So we should thank God every day because we have enough to eat. That's why these children are bowing their heads and saying thank you to God before they eat.

Some Questions to Answer

1. What are some things you are thankful for?
2. Who are some people you are thankful for?
3. Is telling God thank you RIGHT or wrong?

A Little Prayer

Our Father in heaven, thank you for giving me food again today.

A Bible Verse for You to Learn

Thank the Lord for all the glorious things he does. *Psalm 105:1*

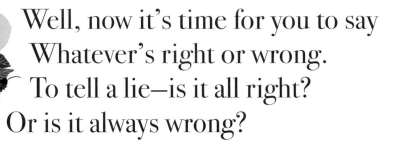

Well, now it's time for you to say
Whatever's right or wrong.
To tell a lie—is it all right?
Or is it always wrong?

Can you see that a cookie is missing from the cookie pan? I wonder where it is? Oh, now I see it! Look what the boy is holding behind his back! His big sister is asking him if he took it, and I'm sorry to say he is telling a lie. He is saying he did not take it. God is very unhappy when his children don't tell the truth. Why is the boy afraid to tell the truth? I think it's because he knows it is wrong to steal. But he should be brave and do what is right and say, "Yes, I took it. I'm sorry." I hope he doesn't ever tell a lie again.

Some Questions to Answer

1. What is a lie?
2. Have you ever told a lie? If you have, you can talk to God about it. You can say, "I'm sorry. Please forgive me."
3. Is it right or WRONG to tell a lie?

A Little Prayer

Dear Father in heaven, help me remember to always tell the truth.

A Bible Verse for You to Learn

You must not tell lies. *Exodus 20:16*

When you are older you will find
That some kids like to steal.
They take some candy; then
they leave.
How sad that makes God feel.

Oh no! I see a girl stealing some candy. She is putting it in her purse instead of paying for it. The lady at the candy counter isn't looking. But someone is watching. God sees the girl doing this, and he is very sad. Did you ever take something that wasn't yours, and did you hide it? I hope not, for that is stealing. If you have stolen something, please give it back to the person you stole it from and say that you are sorry. Then tell God you are sorry. He will forgive you and help you never to steal again. God is glad when we obey him by not stealing.

Some Questions to Answer

1. What is this girl doing?
2. What does stealing mean? Who in the picture is stealing?
3. Is stealing right or WRONG?

A Little Prayer

Dear God, help me never to take things that don't belong to me.

A Bible Verse for You to Learn

You must not steal. *Exodus 20:15*

Be careful, my children;
Don't go with a stranger.
His words may sound good,
But he might bring you danger.

Your parents have probably told you not to get into a car with a person you don't know. Do you know why? It is because some strangers who seem nice aren't nice at all. A stranger might say, "I will give you candy if you ride with me in my car." Or he might say that he will show you his puppies or kittens. But don't go with him. He might be a bad person who would hurt you if you went with him. The best thing to do is to run away from him. Don't talk to him. The girl in the picture is running away from the man who offered her a lollipop. She is doing the right thing.

Some Questions to Answer

1. What is the girl in the picture doing?
2. What should you do if a stranger wants you to ride or walk with him?
3. What would you do if he said he would give you some candy? What if he wanted to show you his puppies or kittens?
4. Is it right or WRONG to go with a stranger?

A Little Prayer

Dear God, help me to run away from anyone I don't know who wants me to go with him.

A Bible Verse for You to Learn

Pretty words may hide a wicked heart.
Proverbs 26:23

See the children talk to God!
He likes it when we pray.
You can't see him, but he smiles
And hears you every day.

What are the children in the picture doing? That's right, they are praying. They are talking to God. God is glad when you talk to him. Do you know why? It's because he loves you. You talk to other people, so you should talk to God, too. He is right here in the room with you, even though you can't see him. What should you say to God? You can tell him you love him. You can thank him for all the good things he does for you. You can thank him for your parents and for your friends. You can tell him about your hurts. God is happy when you talk to him.

Some Questions to Answer

1. What are the children in the picture doing?
2. Does God like to hear you pray?
3. What are some things you can ask him for?
4. Is it RIGHT or wrong to pray?

A Little Prayer

(Say this silently in your heart without using your mouth.)
Dear God, I love you. Help me remember to talk to you often.

A Bible Verse for You to Learn

The Lord . . . delights in the prayers of his people. *Proverbs 15:8*

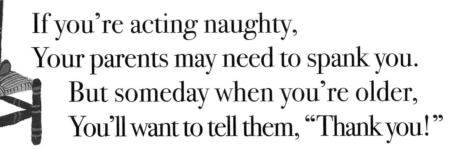

If you're acting naughty,
Your parents may need to spank you.
But someday when you're older,
You'll want to tell them, "Thank you!"

Oh my! What is happening to the little boy? He was taking cleaning bottles out of the kitchen cabinet. His mother told him not to, but he did it anyway. So now the boy's mother must punish him. The little boy will be unhappy for a while, but he will learn to do what's right next time. And he will probably keep on doing what's right when he grows up. After you have been punished, your father and mother should hug and kiss you just like the mother in the picture. Then you will feel good again, and you will know that they love you. They punish you because they want to keep you from doing bad things.

Some Questions to Answer

1. What did the little boy do that was wrong?
2. Do you ever get punished? For what?
3. What are some ways your mother and father punish you?
4. When you do bad things, is it RIGHT or wrong for your mother or father to punish you?

A Little Prayer

Father in heaven, help me to obey and to be kind and good. Thank you that my parents love me so much that they punish me when I disobey.

A Bible Verse for You to Learn

A father punishes a son he delights in, to make him better. *Proverbs 3:12*

TV programs can be good,
But often they are bad.
Don't watch or read of evil things,
For that will make God sad.

Look at the children watching TV. I'm glad they are not really watching it. They are hiding their eyes. They know it isn't good to watch people who are doing bad things. If we watch them, we might decide to be bad too. Sometimes it seems like fun to be naughty, but God doesn't want us to do things that are wrong. He wants us to do what's right and kind and good. It is easier to do what's right when we think about good things. I'm glad one child in the picture is reading a good book. That's better than watching the bad people on TV. The children by the TV should turn it off.

Some Questions to Answer

1. Why don't the children want to look at the television?
2. Do you ever see anyone on TV doing bad things?
3. What do you think you should do when this happens?
4. Is it right or WRONG to look at bad TV?

A Little Prayer

Father in heaven, please help me to always do what's right and kind and good.

A Bible Verse for You to Learn

Happy are those whose hearts are pure, for they shall see God. *Matthew 5:8*

Children, please stop fighting!
Won't you ever learn?
Please don't be so selfish—
Let each other have a turn.

Oh, dear me! Look at the children in the top picture. They are pushing and fighting. They aren't being nice to each other at all. They both want to ride on the rocking horse. But neither of them can play with it while they are quarreling. They are being silly because they aren't sharing. What should they do instead? That's right. They can take turns or even ride the horse together. You can see them riding together in the second picture. Have you ever been foolish by quarreling instead of sharing? I hope not, but if you have been, please don't be foolish anymore. Everyone should have a turn.

Some Questions to Answer

1. What were the children fighting about?
2. Now what are they doing instead of fighting or quarreling?
3. Should you share your toys?
4. Is it right or WRONG to always want your own way?

A Little Prayer

Father in heaven, please help me to share and not quarrel.

A Bible Verse for You to Learn

Only fools insist on quarreling. *Proverbs 20:3*

Do you like helping
Your mother and dad?
It says in the Bible
That this makes God glad.

The Bible tells you to honor your father and mother. What does that mean? It means to be glad about them and to love them. It means to respect them by obeying them. One way to honor them is to help with the dishes. Another way is to help take care of your baby sister or brother. And do it cheerfully! It wouldn't be very helpful if you whined or cried about having to help! So if you are asked to help, say, "OK! I'll be glad to help." And then do it right away. That will make your parents glad, and it will make God glad too.

Some Questions to Answer

1. What are three ways you can help your mother and father?
2. Is it RIGHT or wrong to obey your father and mother?
3. Is it right or very WRONG to pout when your parents ask you to do something?

A Little Prayer

Dear Father in heaven, help me to happily obey my mom and dad and quickly do what they tell me to.

A Bible Verse for You to Learn

Honor your father and mother. *Ephesians 6:2*

It's easy to be polite
  By saying please or thank you.
    Remember to say those words.
    You know it is right to do!

When you ask for something, do you ever say, "Gimme that"? That's not very polite, is it? It is more polite to say, "May I please have it?" And when someone gives you something, it is polite to say thank you. Being polite shows respect. That means you think the other person is as good as you are, or even better. God wants us to respect other people, so he likes it when we are polite.

Some Questions to Answer

1. Point to a child in the picture who is not being polite.
2. Do you see a child who is being polite?
3. Tell some ways you can be polite.
4. Is it RIGHT or wrong to say thank you and please?

A Bible Verse for You to Learn

How wonderful it is to be able to say the right thing at the right time! *Proverbs 15:23*

If someday a boy
Is careless or bad
And breaks your new toy
But feels very sad,
Remember to say,
"It's OK, I'm not mad."

This girl's name is Debbie, and her brother is John. She was careless and broke John's new toy. John started to cry because she did this. But Debbie was sorry about being careless. She told him, "I'm sorry. I didn't mean to do it." Then John stopped crying. He decided to tell her, "It's OK."

Some Questions to Answer

1. What happened in the picture?
2. Did anyone ever break one of your toys or hurt you? Tell about it.
3. Is it RIGHT or wrong to forgive people for bad things they have done?

A Little Prayer

Father in heaven, help me to forgive others just as you forgive me.

A Bible Verse for You to Learn

Be kind to each other, tenderhearted, forgiving one another. *Ephesians 4:32*

Roberto is a little boy
Who puts his toys away.
When Mother says,
"Please do it now,"
Roberto will obey.

This little boy's name is Roberto. He is a happy little boy, but sometimes he doesn't like to put away his toys when it is time to go to bed! One day when a baby-sitter was taking care of him, he thought, *Tonight I won't need to put away my toys because my parents aren't home.* But then he thought, *I should do what my parents want me to, even though they aren't here.* So he is putting his toys away. His parents will be happy when they come home and find everything put away. God is happy too, because Roberto is obeying his father and mother.

Some Questions to Answer
1. What is Roberto doing?
2. What can you do to make your father and mother happy?
3. Does it make your parents happy when you obey them?
4. Is it RIGHT or wrong to do what your mother or father want you to do?

A Little Prayer
Dear God, help me want to do what my parents tell me to.

A Bible Verse for You to Learn
Children, obey your parents. *Ephesians 6:1*

Terry was a little boy
Who had a friend named Chad.
But Terry said his
 friend looked dumb,
And that made Chad feel sad.

The children in the picture are playing soccer. Some of them are having a good time. But two of them are unhappy. Terry is pointing at Chad and making fun of him because Chad missed the ball when he tried to kick it. Terry said Chad looked dumb! Of course, that hurt Chad's feelings. I think we should tell Terry something important. Let's tell him, "Terry, don't say things that hurt other people's feelings. God wants us to be kind to each other and to love each other." I hope Terry tells Chad he is sorry. Then Chad will feel better, and they will both be happy again.

Some Questions to Answer

1. What are the children doing?
2. What did Terry say to Chad?
3. Is it right or WRONG to make fun of other people?

A Little Prayer

Dear God, please help me to be kind to everyone. Help me not to say unkind things about them.

A Bible Verse for You to Learn

Some people make cutting remarks,
but the words of the wise bring healing.
Proverbs 12:18

Getting mad is foolish.
It doesn't help a bit!
Instead, control your temper—
Don't kick or bite or hit!

In the top picture you can see a girl named Julie. She was playing a table game with her sister, Meg. She didn't win, so she knocked the game off the table. Now she won't play anymore. I think she is being a poor sport, don't you? She got mad about losing. But God doesn't want people to act that way. He wants us to learn to be happy even when we lose. In the bottom picture you can see Julie being sorry about what she did. Now she is helping Meg instead of being angry. Julie is learning to control her temper.

Some Questions to Answer

1. Why did Julie knock the game off the table?
2. What should she have done when she was losing?
3. When Julie got mad because she lost the game, was that good or BAD?
4. When Julie came back and helped her sister, was that RIGHT or wrong?

A Bible Verse for You to Learn

A wise man restrains his anger. *Proverbs 19:11*

Shadow is a guinea pig
That likes to run and play.
Keri is in charge of it;
She feeds it every day.

How many pets can you see in the picture? Pets are a lot of fun, but they can't take care of themselves. Do you know that God wants us to take care of our pets? He doesn't want us to forget to take care of them. That would be mean and cruel. He wants us to feed them and clean their cages and give them water. God is happy when we are kind to animals. He made them, and he wants us to take care of them. Are you a good "taker-carer" of your pets? I hope so.

Some Questions to Answer

1. Do you have a pet? What is its name?
2. Can you remember a time when you forgot to take care of your pet? Was your pet sad? What did it say?
3. Is it RIGHT or wrong to take care of your pet?

A Little Prayer

Dear God, thank you for making my pets. Help me to take good care of them.

A Bible Verse for You to Learn

A good person is concerned for the welfare of his or her animals. *Proverbs 12:10*

Please have a little patience!
Don't push and kick and fight.
Sometimes you'll tire of
waiting,
But you'll be doing right.

It isn't fun to wait and wait for your turn, but think what it would be like if everyone wanted to be first! There would be a lot of unhappiness and pushing and shoving and crying. In the picture you can see some children who are being patient and waiting for their turn. But I see two boys who aren't being patient at all. They are arguing over who should get the red car. If you were in the picture, what would you be doing? I hope you would be waiting patiently. God wants us to be patient and fair.

Some Questions to Answer

1. What are the children in the picture doing?
2. Which ones are arguing?
3. What should they do instead?
4. Is it RIGHT or wrong to be patient?

A Little Prayer

Dear Father in heaven, help me learn to be patient and wait for my turn.

A Bible Verse for You to Learn

Be patient and you will finally win.

Proverbs 25:15

"Yes, I'll do it," said the boy.
"I'll do it right away."
But he forgot what he had said,
And he ran off to play.

Have I ever told you about Jamie? He had a "forgetter" in his head!
He'd promise something and then forget about it. His promises didn't
mean a thing. One day he promised to shovel snow. He started to do it,
but then he stopped. He played with his friends and forgot all about
shoveling snow. For a long time after that, Jamie's mother didn't
believe him when he made a promise. Now Jamie has learned to do
what he promised. So his mother believes him. She is happy, and he is
happy too. Remember always to keep your promises.

Some Questions to Answer

1. What did Jamie tell his mother he would do?
2. Did he do what he promised?
3. Can you think of something you said you would do, but then you
   didn't do it?
4. If you make a promise, is it RIGHT or wrong to keep your promise?

A Little Prayer

Thank you, God, for always doing what you say. Help me to always
keep my promises.

A Bible Verse for You to Learn

God delights in those who keep
their promises. *Proverbs 12:22*

Can you do some things better
Than any other kid?
Remember, God is helping you,
So don't start acting big!

In the picture, Sarah is acting like she thinks she is better than all the
other children. She thinks she is the best one in the class. Sometimes
she even says, "I'm better than you are!" She is being selfish and
proud. This is not good. Do you ever act like Sarah? If you do, please
don't do it anymore. If you are especially good at coloring or tumbling
or playing a game, remember it is because God is helping you. So don't
be proud about it. That would make God sad. Say thank you to God
instead of thinking you're so great.

Some Questions to Answer

1. Why is Sarah acting proud?
2. Is it right or WRONG for her to act that way?

A Little Prayer

Father in heaven, thank you for the things I am good at doing.
Thank you for helping me.

A Bible Verse for You to Learn

Pride goes before . . . a fall! *Proverbs 16:18*

A boy grows up, becomes a man, And then he gets a wife. The Bible says that they should stay Together all their life.

Oh, look! It's a pretend wedding! Everyone is happy and excited. Do you see the children's parents standing there watching? Perhaps they are remembering their wedding. They promised to stay together all their lives. God wants them to do this. He is not happy when fathers and mothers leave each other and get divorced. So if you get married, always love your own husband or wife. Don't let anyone else take that person's place.

Some Questions to Answer

1. Does God want mothers and fathers to always love each other?
2. How can you tell that the parents in the picture love each other?
3. If you get married when you grow up, will it be RIGHT or wrong to always love your husband or wife?

A Little Prayer

Dear God, please help mothers and fathers everywhere to keep on loving each other.

A Bible Verse for You to Learn

Husbands, love your wives. *Ephesians 5:25*

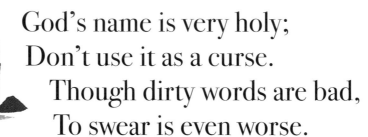

God's name is very holy;
Don't use it as a curse.
Though dirty words are bad,
To swear is even worse.

One of the boys in the picture is saying something very naughty. Two children are holding their ears so they won't hear it. The boy was mad at his blocks and said God's name. But he wasn't thinking about God at all. That was wrong. God says we should never use his name that way. His name is holy. We must respect and honor his name. We must not use it carelessly. You can use God's name when you pray and when you tell others about him. But never use it when you are angry. Please remember this because it is so important to God.

Some Questions to Answer

1. What is happening in the picture?
2. Why are two children holding their ears?
3. Is it right or WRONG to say God's name when you are angry?
4. Is it right or WRONG to use naughty words?

A Little Prayer

Dear Father in heaven, help me to always honor your holy name.

A Bible Verse for You to Learn

Do not misuse the name of the Lord your God. *Exodus 20:7*

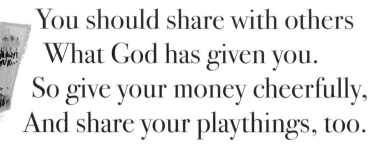

You should share with others
What God has given you.
So give your money cheerfully,
And share your playthings, too.

These children are bringing toys and food to church! Some families do not have enough money to buy what they need. We can show we love God by giving food and toys to those people. We can also give some of our money to God by giving it to our church. Then some of that money will be used to send missionaries to tell children in other countries about God and his love. Jesus said we should not love our money or keep all of it. We should use some of it to help others.

Some Questions to Answer

1. What are the children doing?
2. What will happen to the food?
3. What happens to the money we give to God at church?
4. Is sharing RIGHT or wrong?

A Little Prayer

Our Father in heaven, thank you that we can help people who don't have enough food.

A Bible Verse for You to Learn

Store your treasures in heaven, where they will never become moth-eaten or rusty and where they will be safe from thieves.

Matthew 6:20

Your friends may laugh at you
For doing what is right.
But God is watching you,
So bring him much delight.

I see children doing something very naughty. They are dumping trash out of the trash cans. Now the garbage is everywhere. The children have made the school janitor's job very hard. They think it is fun to be bad. Do you see the boy who won't help them dump out the trash? They laughed at him for being good. But the boy doesn't care. He wants to please God instead of pleasing the children who are doing something wrong. God is glad that the boy is obeying him and doing what is right.

Some Questions to Answer

1. What are the children doing?
2. Do you think God can see this big mess?
3. Is the boy going to be naughty too?
4. If your friends are doing something that's bad, is it right or WRONG for you to help them do it?

A Little Prayer

Dear God, help me to always do what is right, even if other people laugh at me.

A Bible Verse for You to Learn

Happy are those who are persecuted because they are good, for the Kingdom of Heaven is theirs. *Matthew 5:10*

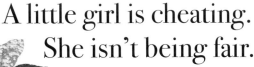

A little girl is cheating.
She isn't being fair.
She sees where kids are hiding,
And soon she'll find them there!

Can you see where all the children are hiding? The girl standing beside the tree is supposed to keep her eyes closed so she won't know where they are. Then she will try to find them. But look at what she is doing! She is watching while they hide. Now she will know where to look, and of course she will find them. She isn't being fair. She is cheating because she is watching instead of closing her eyes. She is not obeying the rules of the game.

Some Questions to Answer

1. Why is this girl watching her friends instead of hiding her eyes?
2. Is cheating right or WRONG?

A Little Prayer

Dear Father in heaven, help me to always be honest and fair, and never to cheat.

A Bible Verse for You to Learn

The Lord hates cheating, but he delights in honesty. *Proverbs 11:1*

Once I knew a little girl
Who liked to storm and pout.
If she's not careful, other kids
Will want to leave her out.

Do you see the little girl who is crying because she is mad? She doesn't want to leave the fair, but her mother says that it is time to go. I'm afraid the girl is making a big fuss about nothing. Do you ever do that? I hope not! God wants you to be happy. Here is what the little girl should do. She should stop crying and think about something nice. She could think about the friends God has given her, or her wonderful family. God has given her so much to be happy about. You talk to her now and tell her to be happy instead of mad. Say to her, "Little girl, please be happy because God loves you."

Some Questions to Answer

1. What are some reasons why the little girl might be storming and pouting?
2. Is it right or WRONG to act like this little girl?

A Little Prayer

Dear Lord, help me not to get mad and cry about nothing.

A Bible Verse for You to Learn

Whatever happens, dear friends, be glad in the Lord. *Philippians 3:1*

The Bible is the Word of God,
Its stories are all true.
If you can't read, I'm sure your mom
Or dad will read to you.

In this picture, Stephen is listening to his mother read him a Bible story. The other children are reading by themselves. They like to read about Moses and King David and Queen Esther. They especially like the stories about Jesus and the wonderful things he did. Jesus made blind people see, and he made sick people well. Someday you will be able to read all of these things in the Bible for yourself. That is something for you to look forward to because the Bible is a special book. God's words will help you know what's right and what's wrong.

Some Questions to Answer

1. Do you have a book of stories from the Bible? If not, ask your mother or father to get one for you.
2. If you know a story from the Bible, tell about it.
3. Is it RIGHT or wrong to read the Bible?

A Little Prayer

Dear God, thank you for the Bible. Help me to read it so I can know and do what you want me to.

A Bible Verse for You to Learn

Your word is a lamp for my feet and a light for my path. *Psalm 119:105*

Sometimes you'll do
What isn't right.
But God has a way
To make it all right.

What I am going to tell you now is *very important,* so please listen carefully. No matter how hard you try, you will sometimes do things that are wrong. These wrong things are called sins. God is perfect and holy, so he must punish sin. But God loves you and sent his only Son, Jesus, to take the blame for your sins. Jesus died on the cross for the bad things you do. Now you can thank him and tell him you want to do everything he wants you to. You can do that because after Jesus died for you, God brought him back to life. Now he is in heaven praying for you.

Some Questions to Answer

1. Why did Jesus die on the cross?
2. What can you do to thank him?
3. Where is Jesus now?

A Little Prayer

Dear Lord Jesus, thank you for taking the blame for my sins. Help me want to do whatever you tell me to.

A Bible Verse for You to Learn

For God so loved the world that he gave his only Son, so that everyone who believes in him will not perish but have eternal life.

John 3:16

About the Author

Kenneth N. Taylor is best known as the writer of *The Living Bible,* which has been revised by a group of biblical scholars to become the New Living Translation. His first claim to fame, though, was as a writer of children's books. Ken and his wife, Margaret, have ten children and numerous grandchildren. His early books were written for use in the family's daily devotions. The manuscripts were ready for publication only when they passed the scrutiny of ten young critics! Those books, which have been read to two generations of children around the world, include *The Bible in Pictures for Little Eyes* (Moody Press), *Devotions for the Children's Hour* (Moody Press), *The Living Bible Story Book* (Tyndale House), and *Big Thoughts for Little People* (Tyndale House).

Some of his recent books include *Everything a Child Should Know about God* and *My First Bible Words: A Kid's Devotional* (written with William O. Noller).

About the Illustrator

Kathryn E. Shoemaker has had broad experience as an art teacher, curriculum specialist, filmmaker, and illustrator. Her published works include twenty-nine books, eight filmstrips, greeting cards, calendars, illustrations for many magazine articles, and numerous educational in-service materials. She is a strong advocate of the involvement of parents in the local schools and used to spend a great deal of time as a volunteer in her children's school. Now she is a volunteer with the Canadian Mental Health Association, the Vancouver Oral Centre for Deaf Children, and the Endeavour Society.

Kathryn is a graduate (magna cum laude) of Immaculate Heart College in Los Angeles. She also studied at Chouinards Art Institute, Otis Art Institute, and Occidental College. She and her two children, Kristin and Andrew, live in Vancouver, British Columbia.

Previous books by Kenneth Taylor that Kathryn has illustrated include *Big Thoughts for Little People, Giant Steps for Little People,* and *Wise Words for Little People.*